D1123323

Simple Machines at School

Gillian Gosman

PowerKiDS press.

New York

For Roger & George

Published in 2015 by The Rosen Publishing Group, Inc.
29 East 21st Street, New York, NY 10010

First Edition

Book Design: Joe Carney
Photo Research: Katie Stryker

Photo Credits: Cover sevenke/Shutterstock.com; p. 4 michaeljung/Shutterstock.com; p. 5 Lisa F. Young/Shutterstock.com; p. 6 Sanchai Khudpin/Shutterstock.com; p. 7 PraxisPhotography/Flickr Open/Getty Images; p. 8 ColorBlind Images/Blend Images/Getty Images; p. 9 Steven Morris Photography/Photolibrary/Getty Images; p. 10 Joe Gough/iStock/Thinkstock; p. 11 Mikko Lemola/Shutterstock.com; p. 12 Kristina Postnikova/Shutterstock.com; p. 13 Steve Cukrov/Shutterstock.com; p. 14 Jupiterimages/Stockbyte/Getty Images; p. 15 Cynthia Farmer/iStock/Thinkstock; p. 16 sodapix sodapix/Thinkstock; p. 17 Christinne Muschi/Toronto Star/Getty Images; p. 18 Jupiterimages/liquidlibrary/Thinkstock; p. 19 Jupiterimages/Pixland/Thinkstock; p. 20 Blend Images - KidStock/Brand X Pictures/Getty Images; p. 21 oksix/Shutterstock.com; p. 22 Pressmaster/Shutterstock.com.

Library of Congress Cataloging-in-Publication Data

Gosman, Gillian, author.
 Simple machines at school / by Gillian Gosman. — 1st ed.
    pages cm. — (Simple machines everywhere)
 Includes index.
 ISBN 978-1-4777-6873-0 (library binding) — ISBN 978-1-4777-6874-7 (pbk.) — ISBN 978-1-4777-6645-3 (6-pack)
 1. Simple machines—Juvenile literature. 2. Tools—Juvenile literature. 3. Schools—Juvenile literature. I. Title.
 TJ147.G6835 2015
 621.8—dc23
                                    2014001269

Manufactured in the United States of America

CPSIA Compliance Information: Batch #WS14PK5: For Further Information contact Rosen Publishing, New York, New York at 1-800-237-9932

Contents

What Is a Simple Machine?

Your school is a busy place. The students learn by exploring, recording, and practicing. The teachers and staff prepare and instruct. The custodians keep the building clean and safe. There is a lot of work to be done in a school!

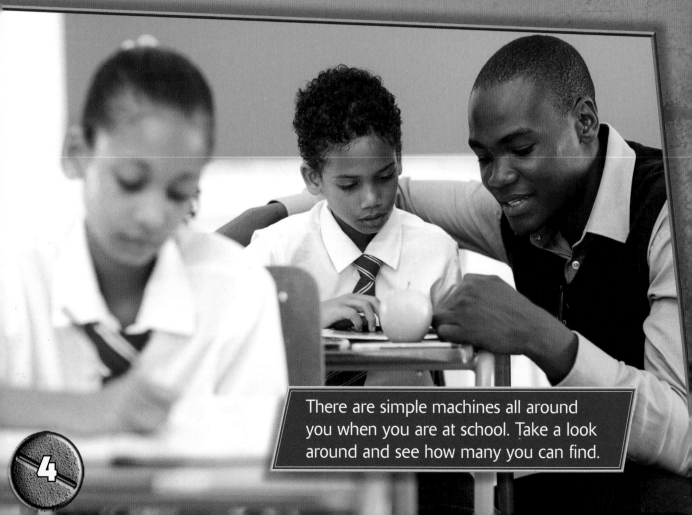

There are simple machines all around you when you are at school. Take a look around and see how many you can find.

If you use a locker at school, you have seen and used several simple machines.

Much of this work is made easier with the help of simple machines. Simple machines **multiply** the **effort** we apply to a job. There are six different simple machines. They are the inclined plane, the wedge, the screw, the lever, the pulley, and the wheel and **axle**. You will find many examples of each in any school.

5

Plane and Simple

Gentle Slope

Steep Slope

The steeper an inclined plane's slope is, the more effort it takes to move something up it.

An inclined plane is a **surface** with one end that is higher than the other. Inclined planes are used to raise and lower objects. It takes a certain amount of work to do a job like this. Without an inclined plane, we would have to apply a great deal of effort all at once. With the help of the inclined plane, we can apply a little bit of effort over a longer period of time.

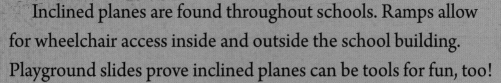

Inclined planes are found throughout schools. Ramps allow for wheelchair access inside and outside the school building. Playground slides prove inclined planes can be tools for fun, too!

Stairs are built on an inclined plane. The slope of the stairs makes them easier to climb and walk down.

It's a Wedge World

You have probably seen tacks around your school. They are used to hold up decorations or flyers. The sharp end of a tack is shaped like a wedge.

A tool with a **narrow**, often sharp, edge is called a wedge. The narrow edge is inserted into or between an object. The effort we put into pushing the wedge is multiplied and **redirected** sideways.

Wedges can be used both to hold objects in place and to separate an object into two. For example, a doorstop holds a door in place, and a nail holds itself in place. On the other hand, any cutting blade, including a plastic knife in the cafeteria or the blade of a paper cutter, separates an object into two.

The workers in school cafeterias use sharp knives like this one to make school lunches. The sharper a knife is, the easier it is to cut with.

Effort

Redirected force

Redirected force

When you turn a faucet on or off, you are using a screw. Inside of the handle, there is a screw. When you tighten the screw, the water turns off. When you loosen the screw, the water turns on.

Any thin **cylindrical** bar with a thread, or ridge, around its length is called a screw. The thread is actually an inclined plane wrapped around the **shaft**. The thread multiplies the effort we apply in twisting the screw, just as an inclined plane allows us to apply less effort over a longer time. The thread lifts the material around it and holds the screw in place.

Screws can be found in almost every room in a school. Screws hold the classroom desks and chairs together. They also keep the caps on the mouths of the plastic water bottles in the cafeteria.

Custodians keep schools in working order. Here, a custodian is using a screwdriver to fix a broken light. The lightbulb also has a type of screw at its base.

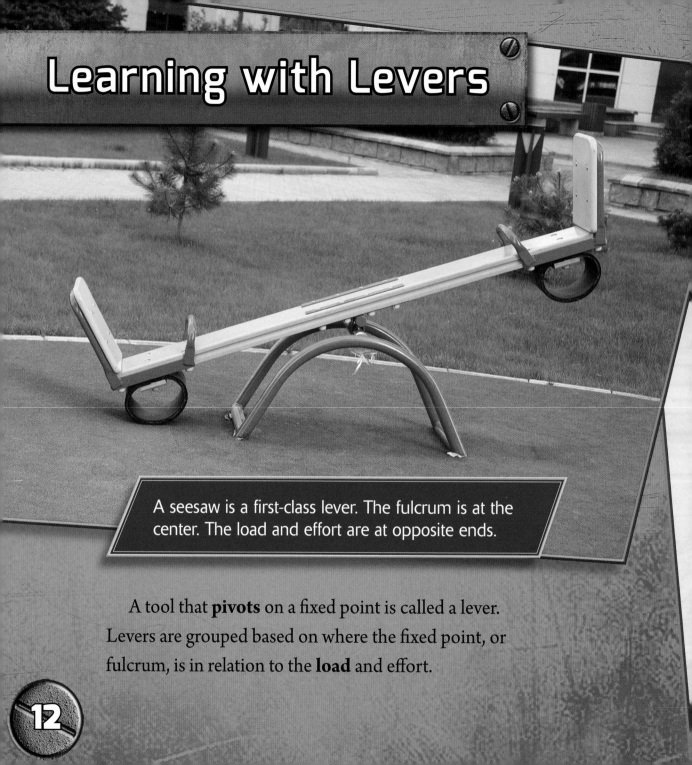

Learning with Levers

A seesaw is a first-class lever. The fulcrum is at the center. The load and effort are at opposite ends.

A tool that **pivots** on a fixed point is called a lever. Levers are grouped based on where the fixed point, or fulcrum, is in relation to the **load** and effort.

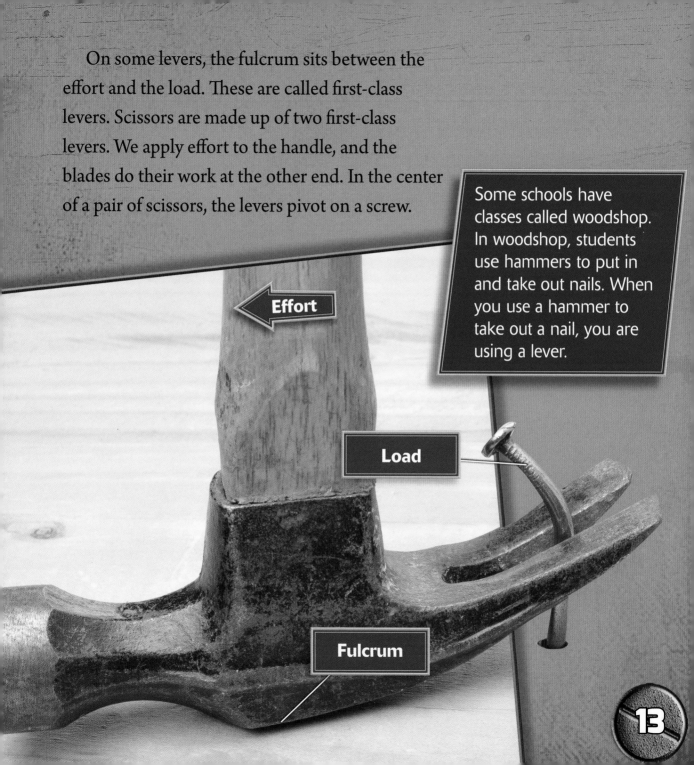

On some levers, the fulcrum sits between the effort and the load. These are called first-class levers. Scissors are made up of two first-class levers. We apply effort to the handle, and the blades do their work at the other end. In the center of a pair of scissors, the levers pivot on a screw.

Some schools have classes called woodshop. In woodshop, students use hammers to put in and take out nails. When you use a hammer to take out a nail, you are using a lever.

Effort

Load

Fulcrum

More to Learn About Levers

Load

Effort

Fulcrum

Your body can be a lever! There are fulcrums all over our bodies. They are mostly joints like elbows, knees, and ankles.

In a second-class lever, the fulcrum is at one end and effort is applied upward at the other end. When you open your classroom door, you are using a second-class lever. The door's weight is the load, and it pivots on its hinges, the fulcrum. You apply effort at the far end, holding the doorknob and pulling it toward you.

In a third-class lever, the fulcrum and the load are at opposite ends, and effort is applied in the middle. A simple classroom stapler is an example of a third-class lever.

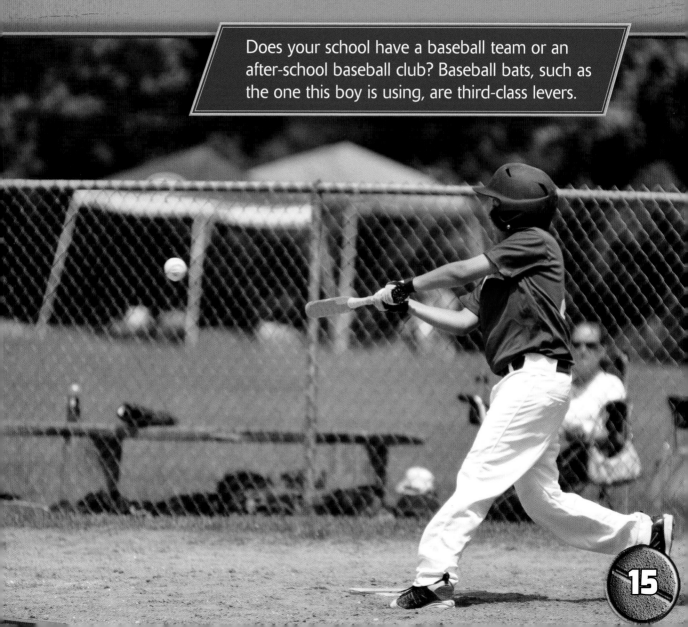

Does your school have a baseball team or an after-school baseball club? Baseball bats, such as the one this boy is using, are third-class levers.

Pulley Pride!

Most US schools have American flags hanging outside. The flag is raised and lowered using a pulley.

A wheel that turns on an axle with a rope, chain, or cable that runs along the wheel is called a pulley. A groove runs along the outer edge of the wheel, and the rope, chain, or cable runs through this groove. The load to be lifted or lowered is attached to one end of the rope, chain, or cable. Effort is applied to the other end. Pulleys can be fixed in place, or they can move along the length of the rope.

Most large curtains, such as the ones in a school auditorium, are opened and closed with the help of pulleys. Theatrical backdrops and some props are also raised and lowered using pulleys.

There are many ropes and pulleys backstage in a theater. They help raise and lower the curtains. They can also help raise and lower scenery.

The Wheel at Work

When you turn the handle of a pencil sharpener around in a circle, you start to turn the interior of the sharpener. When a pencil is inserted, it gets sharper and sharper.

A large wheel attached to a smaller cylindrical rod, called an axle, is a wheel and axle. A standard doorknob, like the one you grip to open the lever that is the door, is an example of a wheel and axle.

The knob is the wheel, and the rod that runs through the door is the axle. By turning the knob, we apply a small force over a long distance. The axle then multiplies our effort, creating a large force over a small distance.

Some kids ride their bikes to school. The wheels of a bike are turned by axles. The axles are turned when the pedals are pushed.

Complex Machines on the Job

Scissors are complex machines that help a lot at school. They are used to make art projects, math projects, or any kind of project that requires cutting paper!

Two or more simple machines used together in one tool are called a **complex** machine. For centuries, people have invented increasingly complex machines!

The scissors mentioned in chapter five are in fact complex machines. Scissors are made up of two levers, two wedges, and one screw. The blades are sharp-edged wedges and a screw holds the two levers together.

A manual pencil sharpener, like the one you may have in your classroom, is another common complex machine. The hand crank is a wheel and axle, the sharpening blades are wedges, and the whole machine is held together with screws.

It is important to keep the sidewalks around a school clear and safe. Shovels are complex machines that clean up snow. They are levers and wedges.

Simple School

We use simple machines at school, at home, at work, and at play. Take a look around your classroom, cafeteria, or auditorium.

Every seat, light fixture, window, and door is made possible by simple machines. Every stapler, sharpener, or pair of scissors does its work with the power of simple machines. While you are learning about simple machines, simple machines are helping you learn!

Simple machines can be found all around your school. In fact, simple machines help us in all aspects of our lives. They are useful at school, at home, and in the great outdoors.

Glossary

axle (AK-sul) A bar or a shaft on which a wheel or a pair of wheels turns.

complex (kom-PLEKS) Made up of many connected parts.

cylindrical (suh-LIN-drih-kul) Shaped like a cylinder.

effort (EH-fert) The amount of force applied to an object.

load (LOHD) Something that must be carried or moved.

multiply (MUL-tuh-ply) To increase.

narrow (NER-oh) Small or thin.

pivots (PIH-vuts) Turns on a fixed point.

redirected (ree-duh-REKT-ed) Moved something in another direction.

shaft (SHAFT) A cylindrical bar.

surface (SER-fes) The outside of anything.

Index

A
axle, 5, 16, 18–19, 21

B
bar, 10
building, 4, 7

E
edge, 8, 16
effort, 5–6, 8, 10, 12–16, 19

H
help, 5–6, 17

I
inclined plane(s), 5–7, 10

J
job, 5–6

L
lever(s), 5, 12–15, 18, 20
load, 12–16

P
pulley(s), 5, 16–17

S
screw(s), 5, 10–11, 13, 20–21
shaft, 10
surface, 6

T
tool(s), 7–8, 12, 20

W
wedge(s), 5, 8–9, 20–21
wheel and axle, 5, 18, 21
work, 4–6, 13, 22

Websites

Due to the changing nature of Internet links, PowerKids Press has developed an online list of websites related to the subject of this book. This site is updated regularly. Please use this link to access the list: www.powerkidslinks.com/sme/scho/

24